A ONE chapter book

The Million Dollar Idea

Where the F**k Do I Start!?!?!

W.T. Hamilton
Your Invincible Power

Copyright © 2018 Your Invincible Power

"When I first connected with WT I knew he was a leader who takes action to make the most out of an opportunity. He knows how to create success and to empower and motivate his clients to do the same. He is an insightful, knowledgeable visionary that gets the job done for his clients."

~ Jim Britt – 13 times bestseller and named as one of the world's top success coaches.

"After 28 years in the speaking industry, when WT and I connected I knew it was a person that saw with vision not sight, that saw a return on investment in one's self. He's gone on to accomplish great things. Learn what he knows. Well deserved!"

~ Jim Lutes – Founder of Lutes International

"WT is a stellar example of tenacity. He is relentless in the pursuit of his passions. He leads with his heart and closes with his head. He's an authentic speaker, dedicated entrepreneur and committed business coach. If you have one person in your corner, make sure it's WT!"

~ Rina Rovinelli – Cofounder of Speaker Slam

~~*

"I've been so fortunate to work with Jim Britt. Can you imagine how amazed and excited I was when I found out that Jim Britt was Tony Robbins' first coach! Jim was also business partners with Jim Rohn!

Then you add the dynamic Jim Lutes, international trainer and mentor to top performers around the world, to the list and you've got a recipe for success.

Learning from these guys helped me really create a life-changing step-by-step, customized action plan that allows my clients to enhance their authenticity, develop mind mastery, create time freedom and build their success on purpose with purpose.

I was also lucky enough to meet and work with Rina Rovinelli and her business partner Dan Shaikh. Rina has been an amazing friend and she has helped me grow leaps and bounds as a speaker. Always giving me honest and helpful constructive feedback.

Since learning and growing with both Jims and Rina I've been lucky enough to learn from Brian Tracy, Sunil Tulsani, Kevin Harrington and the list goes on.

It was by learning the one thing that all these successful people know and that every other successful person knows. It is the one thing that successful people run towards and unsuccessful people run away from.

It's simply this... every successful person has someone that guides them, mentors them and teaches them how to become successful.

That is my mission: to do for you what was done for me."

~ W.T. Hamilton – Author of the One Chapter book series.

No part of this publication may be reproduced, stored in a retrieval system, or transmitted in any form or by any means, electronic, mechanical, photocopied, re-recorded, scanned, or otherwise, except as permitted under Canadian copyright law, without the prior written permission of the author.

Disclaimer:

While the author and publisher of this book has made reasonable effort to ensure the accuracy of the information contained herein, the author and publisher assumes no liability with respect to losses or damage caused, or alleged to be caused, by any reliance on any information contained herein and disclaim any and all warranties, expressed or implied, as to the accuracy or reliability of said information. The author and publisher make no representations or warranties with respect to the accuracy or completeness of the contents of this work and specifically disclaim all warranties. The advice and strategies contained herein may not be suitable for every situation.

Copyright

Your Invincible Power Company (Standard Copyright Licence)

Edition

First Edition

> **ISBN:** 9781717762276
> **Imprint:** Independently published

Published

July 14 2018

Before We Kick this Bad Boy Off…

I want to tell you about how this book series came to be.

Just as this book, The Million Dollar Idea will show you, it all started with an idea. It was a 'what if' moment. I'm sure you've had those kind of moments before. The difference between me and people who only dream about it is, I try to act on as many of those 'what if' moments that I can. I have been able to get myself in the habit, (After some hard work and convincing) to always put as many things into motion as possible.

So in this spirit, the one chapter book series was born. This is the awesome thing about ideas. The more you think about them, the more they grow. The more you put motion into them, the more they become something bigger than you expected, and the more energy you put into it, the more you get out of it.

This is the real magic in having a million dollar idea. It's not the chance to see if you can grow it into a million dollar business, or the laptop lifestyle. The real magic is in the excitement and passion it creates in your life, when you start to see something that started as an idea, really start to grow and take form. This is the power of acting on your ideas.

That is where your power and energy really lives. It's inside your mind. You can wheeled this power to create the things and experiences that you desire. You can build your million dollar idea into something real. Imagine right now, what you can create, just by learning how to really focus on creating and acting on your ideas?

As I started to put the first book, Ask For The Money together, and had the graphic artist create the book cover, my idea machine went into full swing. At that point I already had the core chapters written for this book, and the next one too! I started to expand the possibilities of what this thing could become. I could see in even more detail where I could take it, but not only that, I started to get new ideas that didn't exist for me before, of what I could do with it.

And here's the best part. As I started talking to people about it, opportunities started to pop up for me, in various ways to market and promote the one chapter book series. Things were falling into place and doors were opening up. I was creating movement beyond the idea itself. I was creating energy way beyond the vision I started out with. This is why following through with your million dollar idea is so important, because you never know how far it can take you until you put it into motion, even when you think you know how far it can take you.

This is why I created the one chapter book series. What you are about to learn is, how to create real movement and momentum in your idea. These books are all designed to help you reach your full potential in business and wealth creation. This is the why.

Enjoy.

Thanks, W.T.

Contents

Behind the Scene Info Part Duo........................17

Chapter 3.77 The Million Dollar Idea...............21

Final Thoughts..64

Who is W.T.!?!?...71

Big ups..76

Book by W.T..78

Behind the Scenes Info – Part Duo

As I began to really understand success and failure, I was able to realize one very important factor. The ideas that grow the best have something that the ones that don't are missing. The more I studied and tested this, the more I could see how to take a million dollar idea, and give it the best start I could, to let it grow and expand almost on auto pilot.

Being a consultant means I am constantly meeting people with needs and always providing solutions for them. I create better outcomes than what they can see for themselves. But the more my consulting business grew, the more the types of industries I was helping expanded and grew. I soon found myself in front of a group: the new and struggling entrepreneurs.

I guess it may have been because I was often struggling, and like attracts like.

This was a hidden gift in surprise. Like a Jack in the Box. Helping new entrepreneurs forced me to really get focused on how to take an idea from start to finish, and more importantly, where to start. The beginning is a very important first step. If you start too fast you will run out of energy. If you start to slow you may miss the boat. It all depends on what you are trying to do, and where you are at in your skills, knowledge and attitudes.

So this story starts after I've figured out how to start, and I've started helping entrepreneurs figure out the best way for them to start.

If this is your first time reading a one chapter book here are some of the rules.

1. Read the whole book first.

2. As you read it think about how it applies to you right now.

3. This book is a tool for success. It is not written simply for your love of reading. Use this insight in your life right away.

4. You don't have excuses for why you are where you are, only reasons. This will make more sense as you read the book.

It's time to get started. Congratulations on investing in yourself!

W.T.

Business is serious business.

Chapter 3.77: The Million Dollar Idea

The Million Dollar Idea: Where the F**K Do I Start?

Success always starts the same way. Hey I got this Million Dollar Idea and I know everyone will love it! – And the Journey has begun.

I decided I needed to get serious about my business. I had a business but I wasn't really a business. I was more of an employee working for myself. I had a consistent consulting jig that covered my monthly wages and expenses, but I didn't feel like it was a real business until I realized, if I don't have this consulting contract anymore then what happens.

That's when I had to start looking at my idea book. I have a little book of ideas. Each time an idea pops into my head I try to write it down. Now sometimes they come at inconvenient times, like while I'm in the bathroom doing my business, *(If ya know what I mean.)* Other times it may be while I'm drinking and talking with friends - *You can't always stop to write something down especially when that something may be a variation of what the MoFo you're drinking with is saying!*

So I keep a book of ideas of things that would be awesome to do. I was looking at the book of ideas when my phone rang.

"Hey it's W.T. here." This is the way I always answer the phone, if you've never talked to me on the phone before.

"Hello, my names Bla Bla Bla. I met you at a meetup a few weeks ago and you said that you help people turn their Million Dollar Ideas into viable products and services."

Well this definitely sounded like something I would say to a person at a meetup. It's part of my elevator pitch. Close to the last part of it, just so ya know!

"Yes, that's what I do and funny you called me right now because I'm just looking at my Idea book full of million dollar ideas." I said laughing.

"Got any for me?" Bla Bla Bla's wit was quick.

"Ha ha, remember I said I help you turn your Million Dollar Idea into a product or service?" We both laughed. "And do you know why I would help you?"

"No" he said.

"Because who is going to want that idea to work more than you if it's your idea, your dream?"

"Nice" He said. He then explained to me what it was he wanted to do. I told him that it sounded like he had a good idea and we should meet to discuss it further. I let him know what my rate was and he hesitated.

"If you want to move forward in a way that will bring you real results then you need to let me help you, but if you want to try a few things out and experiment for a while, then you should pass on my help. You may not be ready yet to get serious about what this idea can really do for you. You're investing in your future and how much you are willing to invest will show you how much you should expect in return." I always feel it's important to let someone know up front what they are signing up for.

"I never thought about it like that before. I do want to get this going right now and I really believe in it. It's just a lot of money."

Bla Bla Bla wasn't unlike most people who reached out to me. I know they get nervous when it comes to money so I told him this:

"Do you drink coffee?"

"Yes"

"Do you homebrew or go to the coffee store?"

"Coffee store mostly"

"And you buy a muffin with it too?"

"Yes or a breakfast sandwich" He laughed. He knew where I was going with this.

"Do you buy lunch more than once a week?"

"Yes, I buy lunch almost every day" He said kind of proudly.

"And what do those investments do for you?"

"Huh?" He was a little puzzled. "Those aren't investments, its food. What's the difference if I buy it at the grocery store or at the fast food store?" He asked.

I knew at that moment why Bla Bla Bla wasn't living any type of entrepreneur life yet.

"Quantity and price. You pay extra for convenience. But every dollar you spend is an investment into something. An investment into food, joy, relaxation, entertainment, personal development. There all investments into something, but not everything you invest in brings a return."

"Wow, I see" I knew this was the first time Bla Bla Bla was hearing this. It was the first time he was seeing his money in this way. Every dollar's an investment into something.

Then I said to him, "So what if you cut out some of those things for a while, not forever, but for a time period of say 90 days. What if you looked at some of the things you invest your money into right now, and you curbed the investment so you can give this idea the correct launch it needs to really make it successful. You could do that right?"

"I sure can. That wouldn't be a problem, especially if it means I'm going to be able to create more money with this idea!" I could now hear the excitement in his voice. He just shifted his idea of money from something that can get you things to something you can use to create things. He began to realize you can use money to create wealth.

Every dollar's an investment into something.

"So do you now see how you can free up the money for my help and for the growth of your idea?"

"YES!"

I always like hearing the word YES.

We decided to meet for coffee a few days later.

Coffee is where the dream goes to come alive.

I arrived at the coffee store a few minutes early. Jay Z was playing on the speaker system, 'It's a hard knocks life for us' it's a classic. There were a lot of people there drinking and chatting. You could see right away there were some serious business meeting going on too. I found a table off to the side a little, but still across from another packed table of college students.

I sat down and took a sip of my coffee. Umm Black and Sweet - just how I like it. Bla Bla Bla walked in and sat down. Right away I remembered him from the meetup. I shook his hand firmly in an, I'm going to take care of you and change your life type of way. He looked happy and excited at the same time. *(It could've been the caffeine in the air)*

He asked me, "So where do we begin"

"At the beginning" I said laughing.

"Let's look at the idea from a different perspective. Let's look at it from the sales perspective first. I want you to think about how you would sell it? Is it a digital product? A program or service? What are you selling? Who needs it? Why do they need it? And WHY do they need it from you?"

Bla Bla Bla's eyes were wide open. I could see the wheels turning and coming to a screeching halt. "That's a lot to think about. I need to write them down. Can you repeat them?"

"Sure but my point is, most people start with a website or Facebook page. Logos and content.

Social Media and then, after all that, they start to think about selling. This is how I use to start new ideas, and then sometimes, I found there just wasn't the excitement around it from other people that I felt there should have been, because I didn't develop it with the target audience in mind."

"I see. So you want to start at the end then build the product to fit" I could see the wheels turning again. This time he looked happier and more confident than before. I went ahead and repeated the list for him. He wrote down the questions and started to try to answer them right away.

"I don't want you to figure it all out right now. You need to really think about it. Look at what is out there that is similar to your idea. Start to see how you can do it in a different way and a better way. This is the first step that you need to take. This is where we start."

He liked this approach. I could tell Bla Bla Bla was going to be successful with this because he already knew what he wanted to do, he just needed some guidance in the marketing and approach.

"So tell me what inspired you to want to turn this idea into something more?"

He thought for a moment as he sipped his coffee.

"Money!" He laughed, "And I was tired of working for someone else. I wanted to work for myself, be an entrepreneur."

"So you want financial freedom?"

"Yes, I want to be my own boss."

"Ok that's one thing but why this idea, I mean you can get financial freedom in many other ways. A lot easier than starting your own business. So why this idea?"

"Well, I guess it's because I know a lot about it. I've done this for someone else for years in some way shape or form, but I know this way, my idea will be better, more fun and more rewarding."

"More fun and rewarding for who?"

I could see the wheels turning yet again. A smile grew on his face.

"I see what you're doing. You're getting me to focus on the customer aren't you!?"

"Yes, everything you do is to make someone else's life more fun, essier or better. You get the reward after you help them in some way shape or form with what you do."

"So, that's really where we start isn't it?"

He was feeling very proud of himself for figuring it out.

"Yes and No." I replied to his shock and dismay.

"I need to really get a feel for where you're at right now in your life with this idea. Have you written it down yet?"

"Oh yes, I've written it down, started mapping out how it works, what I can do with it!"

"Have you told your friends and family about your idea?"

"Oh Yeah! They're sick of hearing about it!"

"So you talk about it all the time. You must think about it all the time too?"

"Yes, 24/7."

"And what do you think about in particular when it comes to this idea?"

"All the things I can do with it. The people I can help and how it can improve my life financially as well."

"What if you took money out of the equation? What if you didn't need money, would you still be as motivated to do this?"

"Oh Yeah! I would do this for free if I didn't need money!"

"Are you sure you would do it for free? Would you do it for free right now?"

Bla Bla Bla thought for a minute.

"Ok, maybe I would want some compensation for my time and efforts even if I didn't need the money, why do you ask me this?"

"Because when you start this, you may be working on it for longer than expected before you make any money."

"But I thought you said you can help me turn it into a real product or service in the next 90 days?"

"Yes, I can and you will get some sales but will you break even in the next 90 days? That part is the real challenge."

He sat quiet for a moment thinking. I let this part of the conversation sink in a little bit before I continued.

"If you want to really succeed in your own business, you have to have a real deep passion for what you do. You have to be honest with yourself and you have to be committed to making the idea a success. But you also have to be prepared to work for free to grow your business. It means even the money you make at first will need to go back into the business to really get it started."

"I see, so it's an investment at first."

"Yes, the reality is, the money is not important. What is important is the product or service and how it can benefit people. Do that right and the money will be there. Do it really well and you'll break even and start turning a profit quickly. But there are some rules to success."

"OK what are they?" He was motivated to learn now.

"First you have to be honest with yourself. You have to figure out how much time you can put into this idea right now. The more time you can put into it, the faster it can grow, but you also have to decide how much money you can put into it right now. Then you have to decide, for how long can you do both of these things. What if in 3 months you still need to invest the same amount of time and money into it? Can you do that? What are those numbers? You need to figure out those numbers. These will be your numbers."

"OK and then what?"

"Then with these numbers and the first things I told you to do, we will have the foundation we need to start building your dream into a viable product or service. Sound Good?"

"That sounds excellent. I can't wait!" Bla Bla Bla was filled with motivation and excitement.

Some people would get scared away at that point, and run away, but he knew this was what he needed. A real plan that looked at sales & marketing, short term, midterm and long term resource planning, investment needs, budgets and targeted content.

At this point Bla Bla Bla started to realize he was getting way more value than what he was paying for. He was ready to begin.

***

The next time we met, Bla Bla Bla had done all his homework, and was ready for action. I asked him to meet me at a small English Pub, just off the beat and path, so we could have a little more time to talk and plan. This time he was there before me and had found a nice booth, away from the main area. Sitting in front of him was a beautiful pint of Guinness.

"I gotta get me one of those." I said as I sat down. "So how was your week?"

"It was great! I got so much done with the list of questions you gave me. I wrote the answers all down in my notebook. I figured out what my numbers are and how long I can build this for initially."

He slid his notebook over to my side of the table for me to look at. I read over his answers and looked at the numbers.

"Very good. I like what I see here. You're definitely ready to take the next step."

"What's the next step?" Bla Bla Bla said curiously.

"We need to look at what resources you have right now. Do you have a Social Media presence?"

"I have Facebook and Instagram."

"Do you have a Facebook business page?"

"No, not yet."

"Are you using YouTube?"

"No"

'Website?'

"Yes!"

"Ok. You will need to get the business page set up and link the website to it. Make sure all your Social Media is linked. This will be useful later on in the process. Now we need to focus on what the big idea looks like."

"What do you mean, how to product looks?"

"No, I mean what it looks like as a successful business. You need to start to see it in your mind as already being successful. This is a key step. Now, how you do this is, first write down in detail, the Big Goal. Do you know what the Big Goal is for your business?"

"To be a huge success!"

"Ok that's Capt'n obvious but what does that look like? What does that feel like? When you close your eyes and think about it being a huge success what do you see?"

"Um, I don't know. A big house, nice cars, beautiful women!"

"So you're picturing a Drake video. That's not what success looks like, that's what success can give you. I need you to focus on what success looks like. Is it an event? Maybe having an

Executive office in a high-rise or working on the beach in the Caribbean's. You need to attach a picture of what success looks like and feels like in your mind for one reason."

"What is that?"

"Cause every time you feel like giving up. Every time you think it's getting too hard, you're gonna go to this place in your mind and remember why you're hustling every day. You're gonna visit this mind picture often to inspire and motivate you to make the dream real. You're not going to get comfortable just because you got something that looks close to the success you want, or you got it to kind of work, because you're going to have a clear picture of the goal, and your gonna learn how to focus on it daily, in detail, until you live it in the present moment."

"This is where we really start. We start with the picture of the Big Goal, and then we create the action steps needed to get there. You already have your numbers and you already know why you are building this business, which means, you now have multiple marketing options, so what you need to do now is to focus. Focus on the mind picture. The mind picture of the prize. The thing or experience you'll have once you get there. This is the key step in really creating success in your life. In all areas of your life. I have a program I want you to take that will really help you to get clear on how to do this. How to create the mind picture in detail. How to do this step consistently and successfully so you can apply it to all areas of your life for the rest of your life."

I DM'd him the link to the program.

Bla Bla Bla was amazed at this part of the conversation. He was hearing this way of seeing things for the first time, and it really excited him. He couldn't wait to get started.

"Work on this. Add as much detail as you can to the picture. Follow the lessons in the link too. I'm gonna send you a list of questions, and, the answer to these questions will allow me to create an action plan for you to follow, to bring this dream to life. You are about to begin the work. You are about to build your dream. Your life will never be the same again, so get used to working in coffee shops, bars and hotel rooms, anywhere and everywhere you go, because the world is about to become your office! (And your playground!)"

And, with that, Bla Bla Bla began.

The List of Questions

What is your business?

What does it do?

What do you provide?

How does your business generate income?

What is your intro offer?

Do you have a free trial or giveaway product?

Do you have a big ticket item?

What is your best value offer?

What is your volume offer?

Do you have a funnel product?

How much sales are you making per month?

How much money are you spending per month on your business?

How do you drive sales to your business?

What is your marketing budget?

What part of your business are you marketing?

Where are you marketing?

Who does your marketing?

Who looks after your social media?

What is your social media strategy?

How much time do you spend on creating social media content?

How much time per week do spend maintaining your social media?

How much time a week do you spend on marketing strategies and analytics?

Does your marketing properly position the offers you have?

Do the customers understand the benefits you offer?

When people go to your site or social media is it clear what you do?

Do you have a clear understanding of what your primary business is?

Does your big ticket item or your volume item match your primary business?

What is the one thing above all that you want your business to do right now?

If you could only focus on fixing one part of your business right now what would it be?

Are you able to commit the majority of your business time to achieving this one focus/goal right now & for the next 90 days?

This is the list I use to look at my business at any given time during the year. I use this as a yearly review, and guess what I have found?

Each time I do this assessment, I find that some parts of my business have either expanded into an area that isn't completely clear, or some years I have found that my core message is no longer clear when I look at it in this way. So this exercise becomes a yearly report card for me to see where I am at with my returns on efforts.

Now for Bla Bla Bla, this was an overwhelming task. There was way too many things to think about as he got started, but the reason I had him go through this exercise was, to help him to see all the things that you need to manage in the beginning to launch your business in the right way.

When Bla Bla Bla texted me I knew what to expect.

DM - Bla Bla Bla - WTF!!!

DM - Me - LOL! Don't be scared.

DM - Bla Bla Bla - I'm lost. This list didn't help me at all. I feel overwhelmed.

DM - Me - If a list can overwhelm you what are you going to do when you have to create a business plan, or approach investors, or hire & manage staff?

DM - Bla Bla Bla - OK Captain I get it. Business is serious business.

DM - Me - Let's meet for coffee tomorrow and I'll give you the rundown on getting your business started by the end of the week.

***

The next day we met at a little coffee shop just off of the main street.

It was a cool place. They had a reggae dub mix playing when I walked in. This time I got there before Bla Bla Bla. I sat down and chilled to the music while sipping my coffee.

Bla Bla Bla walked in shortly after and he looked a little flustered.

"So how was the night my friend?" I asked him.

"Not so bad. I looked over the questions again after I calmed down and I could start to see what you were doing."

"That's great." I said as I sipped my coffee. "The reason I wanted you to start thinking about all the things that a business can do was, so you can really start to get clear on what you want your business to do and be."

He listened intently.

"Too many people have a great idea and ambition but never do the hard homework first to know what they are really trying to build. They start with a product and excitement but no game plan when it comes to how they're gonna sell it. Then they wonder why they have little or no sales."

As I spoke, he just kept listening and nodding his head.

"Once you know what you want your business to do, and what you want it to provide, and you understand where the money is going to come from to build it, then you can start to look at all the other areas on the list."

He was still just listening to each and every word I said.

"You have an idea for what you want to do, the passion to do it, and now you are going to create the focus to bring it to life." I sipped more coffee and prepared to let him know how he would start his business.

"Everything starts with the idea. It's in the quality of the idea that success plants it seed. Success can be as simple as bringing the idea from the imagination to becoming a product or service ready to sell. It can be as simple as just being developed into a clear vision of what it can be for the right buyer." I paused.

"You see the idea could just be developed into a turnkey business ready for someone to start. That would be the quality of success that grew from that seed. Or you could produce a better quality of seed. One that has more detail in the idea. One that sees the idea beyond just the development and launching of it. One that factors in the customer experience, the marketing, the benefits and value of the offer. One that understands the monetary and time commitments needed to bring the idea passed its birth and into its triumph."

At this point Bla Bla Bla was on the edge of his seat and fully focused on the possibilities of the business he had in his mind. Finally he spoke.

"So the list is the way I start to plant the fertile seed for my idea to grow into a successful business!" He was more than happy.

"Yes, this is what the list will do for you and more." I sat back and told him how I use the list to help me gauge my yearly progress and assess if I am still being clear to what my business needs to do.

Once I was done I explained to him how I wanted him to start. I said, "I want you to write a full and detailed answer to each of the questions I sent you. Give some real thought to each one and get clear on what you want to do. Think about how much money you can invest into your business on a monthly basis. Once you have completed this, we will meet again and I will give you another exercise. It will be the last exercise you will do before you start building your content and developing your idea into a business."

Bla Bla Bla thanked me and he left to start his homework.

***

A week had past, and it was time to send him the final exercise.

This is what I sent him:

Make a list of all the things that are stopping you right now from achieving your goal or goals in your business. This will be called your reasons.

Beside each one I want you to write a solution. I don't care what the solution is, or how ridiculous it seems to be. Right down a solution for each reason.

Beside each solution group them using A) B) C) D)

A. Represents things you can solve right away.

B. Are things you can solve in a few weeks?

C. Are things you can do in a few months?

D. Are things that will take you a lot longer or can only happen after other solutions are in place?

This will give you the action plan to follow, along with the answers to the questions I gave you last week. You should now have a clear budget to work with, a clear understanding of what your business needs to do, and, now you have an action plan.

Your goal is to make a sale as soon as your content or offer is ready. This will create some cash flow. You may be in the red for a while but if you start focusing on making one sale, just one sale as soon as you are officially open for business, then you will get into the habit of making sales every week that your business is open.

Your sale will be your low priced offer and it can be attached to your intro or giveaway item, but for cash flow, you want to focus on making a monetary sale as soon as you're open. If you are not sure how to do this don't worry I will help you.

Now you are ready to begin. You have the tools to start your business off the right way. It's time to put action to your idea and create your passion business.

Bla Bla Bla was surprised. He said, "That's it!"

"Yes, that's it. You're ready to start."

"That seems too easy." He was a little confused.

"Why does it have to be complicated?" I asked him with real concern.

"I don't know?" He said still a little confused. So I explained.

"There's a simple way and a complicated way to do everything. I always opt for the simple way. Don't make it complicated if it doesn't have to be. Follow this method and start creating your low price point offer. Start creating momentum and cash flow right away. That's what business is. Providing solutions, products, services and things people either need or will really want. What more where you expecting?" I looked at him as he searched for an answer that would make some sense.

He couldn't find one. He knew that he had the blueprint for his success. He just had to start to organize it and scheduling it out. I told him, "Each business is different. Each business owner is unique. If I gave you a pre-packaged plan to follow and it didn't really fit your business or personality then you would grow frustrated with it, and start doing your own thing, and those things would most likely fall apart."

He smiled because he knew it was true. I continued.

"But if I give you all the key ingredients and tools to create your own plan based on how you will work your business, then you have the best chance of succeeding because you customized the knowledge for you. You've created your own success system. Or at least the foundation for one."

He could see that if he did the work to create it, he would be super motivated to make it work. This was the best way to create success. Always to customize the knowledge to fit what you do and how you want your success to be. Never to bend to fit the program because you risk building something that you won't enjoy having.

I told him this, "As you start to move forward with turning your million dollar idea into your business, I will show you how to really build your own success system."

He looked intrigued. "What is that?" He asked.

"It is the system you will use to manage your business and growth. It is the system you will use to manage the expansion of who you are and how you will stay on top of everything, when success starts to move at the speed of life!"

"That's sounds awesome! When do we start?" He was eager.

That's another chapter in your story of success my friend. Get ready, we'll go there soon.

Real soon.

Final Thoughts

Everything starts with the idea. It's in the quality of the idea that success plants it seed.

In this story you learned how to get started in the right way to create the most potential for your success. As you start to build your business in this, way you will create momentum in your business.

Answer the questions that Bla Bla Bla was asked. Consider each as a key part in putting the right ingredients into your seed for success. This is part of building the toolbox for success. There will be hurdles to overcome, no matter how detailed of a plan you make. This is the reality of growth but know that only the ones that face the hurdles succeed.

Let me share with you one of the most important things I did, to help me begin. Now this may not be the most important factor in my success but, it is the most important factor in my beginning. After many attempts, I began to realize that there is no growth without the struggle. I was spending time trying to avoid the struggle. Looking for an easier way to succeed. This was the way I was thinking and I continued to struggle, until I decided to accept the fact that the struggle is a part of the journey.

What this meant was, I had to stop looking for easy. I had to stop wanting easy, and I had to stop chasing easy.

How many opportunities did I miss out on because I quit when it got hard?

How many million dollar ideas did I give up on because I didn't want hard, because I wanted to avoid the struggle?

Too many, that's how many. But once I decided to stop wanting easy and started to look at the challenges as problems I needed to master, knowing that once I mastered those problems, I could achieve that part of the journey, over and over again, no matter how many new million dollar ideas I created.

It was at that moment I knew. I knew I could finish what I started. I would no longer just be a great starter I would become a great finisher too.

This is as important as knowing where to start. You also need to know how to keep going. It will be a mindset transition that will take time to master.

You won't be able to just stop getting frustrated when things get hard, and you may want to chase easy, but know this.

No one ever became rich chasing easy. I never became rich chasing easy. The truth is, easy doesn't pay that well. Work smart. Work hard and work for yourself. That's the best way to achieve your goals, which shouldn't be money, because you can make money doing many things.

The million dollar dream should be to enjoy what you do, have fun doing it, and have people pay you money to do the things you love doing.

Doesn't that sound like a great formula?

You're Welcome!

Use this book as a part of your toolbox for success. Learn from it and implement it in your business right now. The one chapter book series is designed for you to learn how to become a better entrepreneur one chapter book at a time.

Thank you for joining me on this journey of success.

Until Next Time...

W.T. Hamilton

Visit us at www.wherethewindblows.ca

Follow Me on Social Media

In case you didn't know, Instagram is my jam. I post behind-the-scenes footage, marketing, sales insights and motivational videos to help you build success.

I would love to have you join me on Instagram: https://www.instagram.com/w.t.hamilton/

I am also active on Facebook, often posting more in-depth insight and hosting training sessions through my business page. Let's connect!

https://www.facebook.com/wthamiltonauthor

Get A Copy of "Your Invincible Power" motivational book series and more One Chapter Book titles here:

https://www.amazon.com/W.-T.-Hamilton/e/B00YY0S4KK

Copyright © 2020 Your Invincible Power
All rights reserved

Published by W.T. Hamilton

Who is W.T?!?!?

W.T. Hamilton is a business consultant, author, coach who is also an expert in the mindset of success using the law of attraction. He teaches the law of attraction from the non-spiritual side showing people how to apply it to business, and how to create personal success in their lives.

He has written many motivational and inspirational books with his Mom, making them the Unlikely Duo. Now he is expanding his message to utilize his many years of experience in the business world, by creating the ONE Chapter book series.

He is an entrepreneur who has run his own successful management and sales consulting business and continues to work in that field. He has also expanded into coaching and mentoring other entrepreneurs.

At any given time you'll find him on stage sharing personal stories that will motivate and inspire the audience to see life in all the infinite possibilities, as he lives his truths.

He had a dream of speaking on stage, but in the early days, he had a lack of skills to do so until he joined Forest City Toastmasters in London, Ontario Canada, where he crafted the skill of entertaining using motivational messages.

Born in Leister England to an English Mother & a Jamaican Father, then moving to Canada at the age of four, he has a diverse background that has enabled him to really connect with all types of people. Growing up with a multicultural background allowed him to follow his own rules. He wasn't defined by any one culture so he was able to enjoy many cultures, including ones outside of his background.

He became a writer by chance, when learning about the law of attraction, he was turned off by all the spirituality attached to it, and struggled to connect with it at first. He decided to learn it on his own, and started writing about his experience with it, as he learned what worked for him and what didn't.

At the same time, his Mom was planning to write a book about her understanding of this universal law. When she found out he had been writing about his experiences with it too, their first book – Your Invincible Power: Open the Door to Unlimited Wealth, Health and Joy was born; as was this Unlikely Duo.

His Mom was writing from the spiritual side of this universal law, while he was writing from the practical application. This caused some interesting debates and conversations, but it somehow worked, and they still work together on many project to this day.

W.T.'s journey has led him to many great accomplishments, traveling to different cities, to speak, do book signing, coach and enjoy life. He is passionate about sales consulting and success coaching, but also loves to follow his creative intuition, whenever it prompts him.

He is an explorer, a skeptic at heart, an adventurer, and risk taker, always looking to push his limits and challenge his skills.

Believing the comfort zone is where dreams go to die, he is always looking for new ways to test what he knows and what he can do.

From YouTube Channels that he turned into a podcast style show, to launching an iTunes channel on a whim, and creating online training courses because it seemed like a good way to reach more people. You never know what he will do next and neither does he.

He has found the way to use the law of attraction and still be authentic to who he is. He has learned how to use it to focus on success and leveling up his life. This has become his core message and his true passion.

To create a way for everyone to use this method of thinking on purpose, to achieve the things their most passionate about. To live life with passion, and to enjoy what you do every day.

That's who the W.T. is!

Big Ups by W.T.

Big Up to my Mom for working and introducing me to empowerment and the power of our minds. We have created something invincible. Big thanks for your love and for always supporting me in the many adventures of life.

Big Up to my Dad for the encouragement, love and support throughout every step and also for teaching me how to be a dad.

Big Up to my kids for keeping me young at heart and always giving me reasons to laugh, feel proud!

Big up to Fanny Newport (my "ride or die") for loving me as I am and putting up with my crazy life and supporting me in not really growing up too much.

To my extended family who are always throwing love my way. Beers and barbecues for life!

To my many friends – old and new. I'm always thinking about how lucky I am to have people that come into my life for short or long term who make my life better than it would have been had I never met you. You guys and girls get a virtual high five!

And to you! Yeah you, the reader. I give you a special Big Up for investing time and money into yourself. A Big Up for the hunger to make positive change in your life, making your life the best it can be. Keep doing what you're doing. Keep reaching for the top. You got this!

Books by W.T. Hamilton

The ONE Chapter Series

a One Chapter Book
Ask For The Money

a One Chapter Book
The Million Dollar Idea

a One Chapter Book
Really Zuckerburg Really!

a One Chapter Book
The LonelyPreneur

a One Chapter Book
The LuckyPreneur

a One Chapter Book
The Harsh Truths

a One Chapter Book
The Promise

The Your Invincible Power Series

Your Invincible Power
Open the Door to Unlimited Health, Wealth and Joy

Your Invincible Power
How to Remove the Mental Hurdles and Limitations

Your Invincible Power
How to Tame the Ego and Fuel Your Ambition

Your Invincible Power
How to Say Goodbye to the Drama

Your Invincible Power
Incurable ?

Your Invincible Power
How to Create a Positive Relationship with Money

**The Change Book 10
Insights into Self Empowerment**

www.ingramcontent.com/pod-product-compliance
Lightning Source LLC
Chambersburg PA
CBHW030941240526
45463CB00015B/863